MW00414352

THE GIFT OF GRATITUDE

Living with a Thankful Heart

Richard Exley

VALLEW
PRESS

12 11 10 09 08   9 8 7 6 5 4 3 2 1

The Gift of Gratitude
Living with a Thankful Heart
ISBN 978-1-59379-098-8
Copyright © 2008 by Richard Exley
P. O. Box 54744
Tulsa, Oklahoma 74155

Published by Vallew Press
P. O. Box 35327
Tulsa, Oklahoma 74133-0327

DEDICATION

To Jim Stovall
whose wonderful book
The Ultimate Gift inspired me
to live with a thankful heart.

Contents

Introduction...7

Chapter 1: *Thank God for My Salvation*....15

Chapter 2: *Thank God for Family* 23

Chapter 3: *Thank God for the*
Privilege of Prayer.....................29

Chapter 4: *Thank God for My Health* 41

Chapter 5: *Thank God for the Ministry* 49

Chapter 6: *Thank God for Daily Bread* 59

Chapter 7: *Thank God for*
Grandma Miller 73

Chapter 8: *Thank God in the*
Hard Times...............................83

Chapter 9: *Thank God for*
Second Chances 93

Chapter 10: *Thank God for*
His Faithfulness 105

Note to the Reader......................................117

Endnotes 121

About the Author 123

INTRODUCTION

When it comes to happiness, most of us try too hard. With a single-minded determination we set out to be happy and we are sure that given the right circumstances we will be. When we get the right job, when we can afford to drive the right car, when we get married, when we own our dream house, when we can take the vacation of a lifetime—then we'll be happy. Unfortunately, life is filled with people whose experience proves otherwise. One by one they have achieved their goals only to discover that happiness still eludes them.

In truth, happiness is a consequence not a goal. If you pursue it, you will never find it, but if you forget about being happy and simply concentrate on living your life honorable and with a thankful heart happiness will find you. It's like a butter-fly—the harder you try to catch it, the more elusive it becomes. But if you will be still, and wait patiently, it will light on your shoulder.

This truth was driven home to me afresh while reading Jim Stovall's book, *The Ultimate Gift.*[1] But I'm getting ahead of myself so let me go back and start at the beginning.

Morning was just a fringe of light on the horizon as I made my way up the stairs to the ladder that leads to the loft—what I call my upper room. Balancing a mug of steaming coffee in one hand, I climbed the ladder, being careful not to slip. Sitting the mug on a coaster, I made myself comfort-able in my favorite chair and reached for my Bible. When I did I noticed a new book laying on the end table.

On an impulse I picked it up and examined it, admiring the cover and the interior layout. The book jacket was designed to look like a leather bound journal with brass corners and a locking clasp. The pages were buff colored instead of white, with ragged edges to make them look old. Beneath the title were the words, "a novel," which caused me to raise my eyebrows skeptically. It was a small book, barely 150 pages, and I couldn't help thinking that it wasn't really big enough to be a novel; a novella maybe, but definitely not a novel.

Still, I was intrigued so I decided to read a few pages. Before I realized it I was hooked. For the better part of two hours I continued reading and when I finally looked up the sun was laying broad swaths of light across the hardwood floors. By this time I had read enough to know that *The Ultimate Gift* was a rare and special book. Although there was a stack of things on my desk awaiting my attention I couldn't tear myself away. The book was that good!

I could have finished it in a single setting, easy, if I hadn't got distracted. But in chapter twelve Jim Stovall wrote, "When we parted, I asked him why he was always in such good spirits. He told me that one of the great lessons his mother had left him was the legacy of the Golden List.

"He explained to me that every morning before he got up he would lie in bed—or wherever he had been sleeping—and visualize a golden tablet on which was written ten things in his life he was especially thankful for. He told me that his mother had done that all the days of her life, and that he had never missed a day since she shared the Golden List with him."[2]

That's as far as I read. Sticking my finger between the pages, I sat there for several minutes thinking of all the good things in my life. Doing so reminded me that when we remember good experiences we get to enjoy them, not just once, but again and again. Add a sprinkling of gratitude and you have a spiritual tonic that will boost the most despairing soul.

Although I am a thankful person by nature, I had never considered making a golden list. Not something I visualized in my mind but a literal list, written down with black ink on white paper. Picking up a pen, I looked around for my journal but I couldn't find it. I probably should have climbed down the ladder to retrieve it, but I didn't. Instead I decided to write my

golden list on the fly leaf of my Bible.
Unfortunately the fly leaves, both front and
back, were already filled with notes. Not to
be discouraged, I located a page titled
Church Record and decided to use that.

At the top of the page, right under
Church Record, I carefully printed *My
Golden List*. Below that I wrote out James
1:17: "Every good gift and every perfect
gift is from above, and cometh down from
the Father of lights, with whom is no vari-
ableness, neither shadow of turning"
(KJV). That was my way of acknowledging
that every good and worthwhile thing in
my life was a gift from God.

The hardest thing about making my
golden list was limiting it to ten items.
Once I began to take inventory I realized
just how blessed I was. Don't misunderstand me; my life wasn't perfect, still isn't
not by a long shot. Like everyone else I

have had disappointments and challenges to contend with. Our daughter is battling a chronic illness, my father passed away a few months ago, and we have had some financial concerns. Still, these things seemed to pale in comparison to the richness of God's blessing, and I felt my heart lift as I focused on His goodness.

Maybe you should pause right here and take a few minutes to remember your blessings. Instead of thinking about your problems try focusing on God's provision. Remember a specific time when He provided for you. Relive that experience, marveling anew at His generosity and faithfulness.

How do you feel now? Better, I'm sure. More relaxed and confident. Focusing on the goodness of God does that. It encourages our faith and makes us optimistic about the future.

Now you are ready to surrender your present needs and concerns to Him. "Do not be anxious about anything, but in everything, by prayer and petition, *with thanksgiving,* present your requests to God. And the peace of God, which transcends all understanding, will guard your hearts and your minds in Christ Jesus."[3]

In the next few pages I'll share my golden list with you. My purpose in doing so is quite simple—I hope to inspire you to make a golden list of your own. Beyond that I want to remind you that in every situation we have a choice. We can complain about what we don't have and succumb to despair, or we can give thanks for what we do have and experience the peace of God that transcends all understanding.[4]

Chapter 1

THANK GOD FOR
MY SALVATION

After sorting through all the things I had to be thankful for, I realized that one thing stood out above all the rest—my salvation. The other things on my golden list are in no particular order but this is definitely number one. It is the one thing for which I am most thankful, the one thing that gives meaning to everything else in my life.

Although I have lived a fairly decent life by society's standards, by God's law I am a transgressor. I am guilty. There are no mitigating circumstances, nothing I can say in my defense. I have been judged and found wanting. I have sinned and I am under a sentence of death—eternal death. There is absolutely nothing I can do to save myself. But what I could not do for myself, God did for me. "…God demonstrates his own love for us in this: While we were still sinners, Christ died for us."[5]

As a new believer I accepted Jesus' sacrificial death and the salvation it provided without giving it much thought. I was deeply moved by His suffering and death but I never stopped to ask myself why He had to die. As I matured in the faith, I began to wonder why it had to be that way. I mean, why couldn't God just forgive my sins without making Jesus suffer? He's God after all and He can do anything, can't He?

No, He can't.

There's one thing He cannot do—He cannot betray His character. He cannot be untrue to Himself and that's why Jesus had to suffer and die. Being absolutely just God could not allow a single sin to go unpunished; nor could He forgive a solitary sinner until His justice was fully satisfied, until every sin—past, present, and future—was punished.

But justice is just one part of God's eternal character. He is also a God of love and mercy. Being merciful, He could not turn His back on Adam's lost race without betraying that part of His character. Because of who He is, God was compelled to satisfy both His justice and His mercy, hence His dilemma. How could He be both just and merciful? How could He forgive Adam's sinful race without betraying the just demands of His holy nature? Moreover, how could He punish humanity's sins without denying His love and mercy?

The Cross was the only answer, for in the Cross both God's mercy and His justice would be fully vindicated. Through His sacrificial death, Jesus manifested God's unconditional love even as He suffered the full penalty for the sins of all humanity. When He died on the Cross He satisfied the just demands of God's righteous character thus making it possible for God to forgive our sins and still be true to Himself.

Here's how it works. God took every sin—past, present, and future and imputed them to Jesus. In that moment, as far as God was concerned, Jesus was the greatest sinner in time or eternity and He proceeded to discharge on Him the full weight of His unmitigated wrath. The ultimate punishment for sin is separation from God, a punishment Jesus suffered when the Father forsook Him during the three hours of noonday darkness that shrouded the earth that fateful day. Alone in the darkness Jesus cried, "My God, my God, why have you forsaken me."[6]

He received no answer, just silence as cold and still as death. But if we were to ask Father God that same question He would answer us. He would say, "I did it for you. I punished Jesus so I would be free to forgive you. I rejected Him in order to reconcile you unto Myself. I made Him to be sin so that you might be made the righteousness of God in Him."[7]

When I think of the great lengths to which God has gone to make provision for my salvation, when I think of what it cost Him, I am nearly speechless. From the deepest part of my being I praise Him.

With an overflowing heart I exclaim, "Thank God for my salvation!"

Thank God that He did not deal with me as my sins deserve or repay me according to my iniquities. "For as high as the heavens are above the earth, so great is his love for those who fear him; as far as the east is from the west, so far has he removed our transgressions from us."[8]

Thank God that His love is everlasting and His mercies never fail. They are new every morning.[9]

Thank God that Jesus did not come into the world to condemn the world but that through Him the world might be saved.[10]

Thank God that whoever believes in Him shall not perish but have eternal life.[11]

Thank God that when we confess our sins He is faithful and just to forgive us and to cleanse us from all unrighteousness.[12]

Thank God that Jesus endured the shame of the Cross so that we never have to bear the shame of our sins.[13]

Thank God that there is no condemnation for those who are in Christ Jesus.[14]

Thank God that I have been made the righteousness of God in Him.[15]

> "Praise the Lord, O my soul;
>   all my inmost being, praise his
>   holy name.
> Praise the Lord, O my soul,
>   and forget not all his benefits—
> who forgives all your sins
>   and heals all your diseases,
> who redeems your life from the pit
>   and crowns you with love
>   and compassion…."[16]

All the days of my life I will thank God for my salvation and praise His holy name!

Chapter 2

Thank God for Family

After my salvation nothing is more precious to me than my family. I'm eternally grateful to God for my wife, for my daughter and her husband, and for my two wonderful grandchildren. I thank Him for my brothers and for my sister, as well as my nieces and nephews. Still when I think of family my heart turns naturally to Mom and Dad, to the ones who gave me life and willingly sacrificed their present to give me a future.

During the closing months of WW II, the man who was to become my father began exchanging letters with a beautiful, but timid, eighteen-year-old woman named Irene. They could have hardly been less alike. She was a true innocent, having never traveled more than ten miles from her birthplace in northeastern Colorado, while he was a Navy man having spent much of the war stationed in Hawaii. As the war was winding down in the fall of 1945 he was reassigned to Corpus Christi, Texas, and given a two-week furlough. Determined to find out if that dark-eyed beauty was as pretty as her picture, he made his way to Sterling, Colorado.

Of course it was "love at first sight" and after a whirlwind courtship they were married on November 7, 1945. Thirteen months later the Lord blessed them with their first child, a dark-haired little boy whom they named Richard Dean Exley. When I was barely ten days old they wrapped me in blankets and carried me to church, walking nearly three miles through the December cold. I've been in church ever since and thinking about it now, I'm nearly overwhelmed with gratefulness. Thank God for parents who gave me such a rich spiritual heritage.

Although Dad was a hard worker my childhood was spent on the ragged edge of poverty. Shortly after the folks married Dad went into the water well drilling business, but he could never make a go of it. He was under capitalized and his ancient equipment was badly worn and kept breaking down. The thing that finally did him in was a job-related injury, which laid him up for weeks. Without insurance or worker's compensation it put him out of business. Refusing to declare bankruptcy, Dad and Mom spent the next several years digging out of debt.

Although we were poor I don't think I realized it until years later, when I was nearly grown. For all of the things we lacked there was never any shortage of love, making it nearly impossible for me to feel deprived. There were hints though that couldn't be ignored, especially in retrospect. For instance, we had to make a gallon of milk last seven days and there were four of us kids. I was married and out on my own before I ever had a second glass of milk with a meal. Still, like I said, it's hard to feel poor when you live in a home filled with love.

As a boy, Saturday was my favorite day of the week, Saturday afternoon to be exact, and not just because we were out of school either. Every Saturday Momma baked and by mid-afternoon the house was filled with the rich aroma of fresh baked goods—homemade bread, fruit pies, and hot cookies. I tell you the truth; a kid could get drunk on smells like that!

Every Saturday afternoon Momma would give us a half glass of milk and a hot cookie after telling us to shuck off our shoes. While we feasted on hot cookies and cold milk she would shine our shoes and place them against the wall, on the colored funny papers, in the corner of the kitchen. As far as she was concerned it would have been sacrilegious for us to go to church if we weren't looking our best. After all, we were going to see the "King" and it was a matter of respect.

After supper on Saturday evenings we all took baths and shampooed our hair before reconvening around the kitchen table to study our Sunday school lessons, memorize our memory verse, and prepare our hearts for Sunday worship. Dad and Mom decided early on that church attendance took precedence over everything else and there was one question that was never asked at our house: "Are we going to church?" If the church doors were open we were going. It didn't matter what kind of service—Sunday school, youth service, prayer meeting, Bible study, or revival meeting—we were there. That may sound restrictive to you but it was liberating for us. Having settled that issue once and for all we were spared the repeated arguments common to so many families.

Thanks in large part to the godly home into which I was born, I have been spared many hurtful experiences. Because of the spiritual values my parents imparted to me I was never tempted to indulge in the kind of activities that have derailed so many. Instead, I have spent my entire life in the work of the Lord and as a result I am a greatly blessed man. I didn't do anything to deserve it and I certainly didn't earn it. It is all God's doing and I will give Him thanks this day and every day.

Chapter 3

THANK GOD FOR THE PRIVILEGE OF PRAYER

Prayer is number two on my golden list and while I am truly thankful for the privilege of prayer I must confess that I've never been very good at it. My mind wanders. I get distracted, or I put off praying until the demands of the day crowd it out. Over the years I've tried any number of things to improve my prayer life—joining a prayer group, writing out my prayers, keeping a prayer journal—and while they work for a time I soon find myself slipping back into my haphazard way of praying. It embarrasses me to tell you this, but I don't feel I can write about the privilege of prayer without coming clean about my own inaptitude.

I know all the things I should do— reserve a special place to meet with God, have a set time for prayer, make myself accountable to another person (preferably someone who has mastered the discipline of prayer), and most of all pray whether I feel like it or not. After all, we learn to pray the same way we learn to ride a bike—by doing it. I know the importance of praying the Scriptures and of praying God-centered prayers rather than need-centered prayers. My problem isn't knowledge but discipline. I know all I need to know about praying. I just don't pray as faithfully as I should.

Although I've received many remark-able answers to prayer, which we will get to in a minute, I still grow weary of praying when my prayers seem to be making no apparent difference. I mean, why pray if nothing changes. Reminding myself that when one fills a pond the first hundred truckloads of rock disappear under the surface of the water without leaving a trace helps some, but I still have to struggle with discouragement. Reminding myself that the primary purpose of prayer is not petition … but relationship, about spending time with the Lord, helps some. Unfortunately, it is often as hard for me to sense His presence as it is for me to see His answers.

If prayer is so frustrating, you may be wondering, why do I continue praying? I'm sure a sense of duty has something to do with it, but it is more than that. At the core of my being I have a heart hunger for God, a yearning to know Him and be known by

Him. It is an "itch" that only prayer can scratch. I may not be very good at prayer, I may even stray from it from time to time, but always I am drawn back. What breath is to my body prayer is to my spirit. Without prayer I simply cannot survive.

Of course, prayer is not all discipline and frustration. In fact, there are times when prayer seems as easy as breathing and just as natural. The Holy Spirit comes upon us and we are moved into a spiritual realm where prayer has an energy of its own, a strength that seems to literally carry us. Now prayer takes on a life of its own. With absolutely no effort we spend extended time in His presence without once being conscious of the clock. When the Spirit lifts we are amazed to realize that two or three hours have passed, maybe longer.

While I wish every moment spent in prayer could be like that I have to acknowledge that such times are the exception and not the rule. It is also interesting to note that there seems to be no correlation between the spiritual and emotional intensity of my prayers and their effectiveness. If the truth be told my fumbling, halfhearted prayers seem to produce as many answers as those holy moments when prayer takes on a life of its own. I can only conclude that the power of prayer rests in the God to whom I pray and in nothing else.

Once, I and two companions were caught in a blinding rainstorm while fishing in the Gulf of Alaska. When the pounding rain finally subsided a thick fog settled in reducing our visibility to just a few feet. Unable to see any landmarks and without a compass to guide us we

became disoriented and lost our way,
although we refused to admit it. Blindly
we forged ahead for three hours or more.
From time to time I could hear the
pounding of the heavy surf as it crashed
on the rocky shoreline of an island
rendered invisible by the fog and a
disconcerting sound it was. If we miscal-
culated our course, and ran aground on
one of the hundreds of uninhabited
islands that make up the Alexander
Archipelago, those jagged rocks would
shred our rubber craft in seconds, plung-
ing us into the frigid waters and pounding
surf. Belatedly I decided to pray.

Hardly had I finished praying before
a fishing trawler emerged from a fog bank
on a course that would intersect ours.
Frantically we began waving to attract the
captain's attention. Instantly the throb of
the fishing boat's powerful engine fell off

and the captain brought her alongside our rubber raft. We explained our situation and asked him if he could direct us to Sitka. To our chagrin he told us that we were heading directly away from our destination. Nodding toward the horizon, where mountains draped in gray mist could now be seen against the sky, he told us, "Keep those mountains to starboard and you should reach Sitka in about thirty minutes."

A half hour later we were tying up at the dock. Once more the sea was calm and the sun was shining brightly. As peaceful as it now was, it hardly seemed possible that we were ever in any real danger, but I know we were. In fact, had it not been for God's faithfulness to answer prayer we might well have been lost somewhere along the Inside Passage that links Sitka with the lower forty-eight states.

Some may scoff at the thought that the sudden appearance of that fishing trawler was an answer to prayer, but I am convinced it was. God, who is beyond time, as we know it, has promised that "before [we] call [He] will answer; while [we] are still speaking, [He] will hear."[17] Knowing where we would be at that precise moment, and knowing that I was going to pray for help, God had already arranged to have that fishing trawler in position.

That's just one of countless times God has intervened on my behalf in response to my desperate prayers. Of course, He is no respecter of persons and I am sure He has done the same for you. Why don't you take a minute right now and remember a specific time when God answered prayer on your behalf. You may have prayed for wisdom to make a decision and suddenly after weeks of indecision the way seemed so clear. Or perhaps, you prayed for financial provision and God supplied in the most unexpected way. Or maybe, you prayed for a physical healing and God intervened.

Initially it is easy to see the hand of God at work in your life, but as time goes by the enemy will tempt you to doubt the power of prayer. He will suggest that what you are calling an answer to prayer is really nothing more than a coincidence, that things would have worked out the same way whether you prayed or not. Perhaps, but experience has taught me that these "remarkable coincidences" occur with significantly greater frequency when I pray.

Are you facing a huge challenge in your life right now, some situation or circumstance that feels overwhelming to you? Don't despair! Every time you breathe a prayer in Jesus' name, Almighty God gives you His undivided attention and there is nothing too hard for Him. "Let us then approach the throne of grace with confidence, so that we may receive mercy and find grace to help us in our time of need."[18]

One final thought: Prayer is a privilege. When I was just a young man preparing for the ministry, prayer was greatly emphasized. I was left with the distinct impression that it was an obligation. As I matured in the Lord, I came to realize that it was more a discipline than an obligation, a discipline that would one day turn into a delight. Now, after more than forty-one years in active ministry, I am finally coming to understand that prayer is, first and foremost, a privilege. Try to get an audience with some earthly dignitary and what do you think your chances are?

Probably not very good. But every time we whisper a prayer in Jesus' name, God promises to meet us there. Think of it. The infinite, almighty, sovereign God promises to meet with us every time we come to prayer. Now that's a privilege!

Chapter 4

THANK GOD FOR
MY HEALTH

I praise the Lord for my health! I am a grandfather and have never been seriously ill a day in my life. In fact, I am almost never sick. Although medical statistics indicate that most people have two or three colds a year, I seldom have one—maybe once every five or six years, sometimes not that often. And I haven't been sick enough to "lose my cookies" since I was twenty-two years old. I can take no credit for my good health. It is a gift from God, unearned and undeserved but one for which I am especially thankful.

I wish I could tell you that I exercise regularly and that I eat the way the health gurus tell us to eat but I can't. If the truth be told we have a saying at our house, "If it's fat free throw it out." Don't misunderstand me. We aren't deliberately unhealthy in the way we eat; but we are a throwback to an earlier generation who ate lots of fruits and vegetables, as well as meats, cheese, and whole milk. We don't count calories or fat grams but we do try to eat in moderation, at least most of the time.

I've never been into exercise for exercise sake but I've always enjoyed sports. Rather than jogging or bicycling, I played basketball. Instead of working out, I played vigorous games of racquetball three times a week, usually with men ten or fifteen years younger than me. When I left the pastorate at the age of forty-six and moved into a cabin located on Beaver Lake, twenty-five miles from the nearest town, I gave up both basketball and racquetball. Now Brenda and I walk the rugged shoreline or climb the steep hills surrounding our cabin. With two wood burning stoves, we are always in need of firewood so I get plenty of exercise with a chain saw and a log splitter, not to mention all the wood I have to carry when the temperatures drop below freezing.

Still, having said all of that, I want to repeat, "My good health is not so much a result of my lifestyle as it is a gift from God, unearned and undeserved." And, I've lived long enough to know that the condition of my health could change tomorrow. I don't expect it to change, but neither am I naïve enough to think that I will never have to face any of the health challenges that are common to so many others.

So what will I do if I am suddenly stricken with a serious or even life-threatening illness?

That's a good question and one I will try to answer as truthfully as I can. Of course, no one knows how they will respond until the imagined scenario actually happens but here's what I have purposed in my heart to do. I will praise the Lord for the promise of healing.[19] As I have praised Him during the seasons of good health, so I am determined to praise Him should sickness strike.

And if I am not healed, I have determined to praise Him for the promise of His presence.[20] As surely as He was with me when I was blessed with extraordinarily good health, so He will be with me should my health fail. He will never leave me nor forsake me, and as long as He is with me I can bear all things. This is the ultimate truth of Christianity. It does not make us immune to life's inevitable hardships and tragedies, but it does empower us to live triumphantly, no matter what challenges may confront us.

And when I inevitably face death, as we all shall, I am determined to praise Him for the promise of eternal life. For I know that if I am absent from this mortal body I will be present with Christ[21] and that for me to live is Christ, but to die is gain.[22]

When my father went to be with the Lord at the age of eighty-three, he went with a smile upon his face. Forty-eight hours before his death he went into a coma from which he awakened only momentarily at the very end. Mother was lying on the bed beside him, as was my sister. My two brothers and I were on the other side of the bed. Bob was standing at the head of the bed softly stroking Daddy's hair, while Don was standing beside him holding Daddy's hand. Standing between them and just a little behind, I had a clear view of my Father's face. For days he had lain with his head back and his mouth wide open as he labored to breath, but as he drew his last breath he closed his mouth and opened his eyes. Focusing on something only he could see, Daddy smiled and tried to sit up, and then he was gone.

Thinking about it now, I am sure Jesus came for Dad just as He promised He would, "…if I go and prepare a place for you, I will come again, and receive you unto myself; that where I am, there ye may be also."[23] There was no death angel in that room, just the Lord of life coming to call my father to his eternal reward.

Even as I praise the Lord for my health I am also asking Him to let me live until I die. I never want to become a burden for anyone. May the Lord allow me to remain healthy and productive as long as I live and when I have finished my course, accomplished all He has set before me, I am asking Him to take me home. It may not happen that way, but that is my prayer. Regardless, I am determined to praise Him in all things for He is truly worthy of praise!

Chapter 5

THANK GOD FOR
THE MINISTRY

I was just thirteen-years-old and kneeling between the first and second pew in the South Houston Assembly of God church when God called me to preach. There was no audible voice, no vision, but the Lord's call could not have been clearer. When I arose from the place of prayer my destiny was set. The details, of God's plan for my life, continue to manifest themselves these many years later, but the direction was set that night. I was a called man, set aside by God for the work of the ministry. As the Bible says, "No one takes this honor upon himself; he must be **called** by God...."[24]

My first sermon was a disappointment to me and everyone else who heard me. For eight minutes I preached in a monotone, staring at the wall to my left, never daring to make eye contact with the congregation. Later I learned that Brenda's mother told her husband that she had grave doubts about whether I would ever develop into a preacher. Of course, I was only sixteen-years-old and without any formal training so I guess I really shouldn't have been so hard on myself.

Embarrassed though I was by my inaptitude, I never doubted God's call. With renewed determination I plunged ahead. Soon Brenda and I were leading children's church at our home church, and it was there that I discovered I had a gift for storytelling. Week after week the children seemed to hang on my every word and when I invited them to receive Jesus as their Savior many of them responded. At seventeen years of age I was elected president of our youth group and thereafter I found myself preaching almost every week. I organized a coffee house ministry, street witnessing, and participated in services at the county prison farm where I sometimes preached. Soon I began receiving invitations to preach youth rallies and revival meetings. God was confirming His call on my life.

The joyous excitement I felt in those early days has not waned. After forty-five years of active ministry my enthusiasm is undimmed. I'm not tired, or burned out, or discouraged. In fact, I love the ministry more today than ever before. As long as God gives me strength I plan to walk through every door He opens and to do everything He calls me to do. Truthfully, I'm more passionate about ministry now than I've ever been. I'm not looking for a place to stop, just for wisdom and guidance to do all He puts before me!

I have spent all of my adult life in the work of the Lord and during more than four decades of ministry I have been privileged to serve as the senior pastor of four wonderful churches. It was an honor to serve these congregations in ways both great and small. I have dedicated their babies and baptized their children, performed their weddings, and preached their funerals. We have celebrated life's blessings together and grieved its painful disappointments, always finding God's strength sufficient. I cannot imagine any other vocation that would have afforded me such a rich diversity of experiences.

Truly, I thank God for allowing me to serve in ministry.

Although Brenda and I have been blessed beyond anything we might have imagined, it hasn't always been easy, especially during the early years. During the first eight or nine years, we experienced some painful rejections and suffered a number of devastating disappointments. There's nothing to be gained by delving into the painful details, but let it suffice to say that at one point, early in 1975, we almost gave up. It simply seemed there was no place for us in the ministry and I couldn't help wondering if I was washed up at the age of twenty-eight.

We were without a church and desperately short on funds. Although I continued to send out resumes not a single pulpit committee seemed interested. Weeks turned into a month, then two, then three without a single positive response. During those dark days two things sustained me— my call to ministry at the age of thirteen and a passage of Scripture from Isaiah that the Lord had impressed upon my mind while I was praying.

> "I took you from the ends of
>   the earth,
>   from its farthest corners I
>   called you.
> I said, 'You are my servant';
>   I have chosen you and have not
>   rejected you.
> So do not fear, for I am with you;
>   do not be dismayed, for I am
>   your God.
> I will strengthen you and help you;
>   I will uphold you with my
>   righteous right hand.
> All who rage against you

> will surely be ashamed
>   and disgraced;
> those who oppose you
>   will be as nothing and perish.
> Though you search for your
>   enemies,
>   you will not find them.
> Those who wage war against you
>   will be as nothing at all.
> For I am the Lord, your God,
>   who takes hold of your
>   right hand
> and says to you, Do not fear;
>   I will help you."[25]

Again and again I returned to that passage, clinging to it the way a drowning man clings to a lifesaver. "…I called you…. I have chosen you and have not rejected you. So do not fear, for I am with you…."[26] God had called me. He had chosen me and He had not rejected me; that's what the Bible said.

And, as the ensuing years have proven, God was faithful to His call and to His Word. We finally received a call to serve *The Church of the Comforter* in Craig, Colorado, and we have never lacked a place to preach from that day to this. In the past thirty-two years ministry has taken us to all fifty states and more than twenty foreign countries. God has enabled me to publish thirty-one books to date and for a number of years I hosted a live, nationwide call-in radio program called *Straight from the Heart*. I have preached to crowds as large as 14,000 and to a handful of people in a remote village in Bangladesh.

While serving as the senior pastor of Christian Chapel in Tulsa, Oklahoma, we experienced a season of signs and wonders and prophetic ministry, the likes of which I have never seen anywhere else except in Argentina.

Through the ministry I have met some of the most remarkable people, had some of the most extraordinary experiences, and I can't imagine any other life so richly fulfilling. Truly I can't help but say, "Thank God for the ministry!"

Chapter 6

THANK GOD FOR
DAILY BREAD

Some years ago our ministry was experiencing some financial difficulties. For several months we experienced a negative cash flow and our reserves were nearly depleted. I was reluctant to share our need with anyone but the Lord. Years earlier He had spoken to me, impressing upon my heart that if I would talk to people about Him, and talk to Him about money, all our needs would be met.

Unfortunately, it didn't seem to be working this time and I had reached the point where I was seriously considering sharing our situation with two of our most faithful supporters. They were both in a position to help us and I had no doubt that they would if I made our needs known. As I was prayerfully contemplating this the Lord seemed to speak to my heart. Quietly He asked, *"Do you really think they care more about you than I do?"*

Having been gently rebuked, I determined to trust the Lord. Instead of focusing on our financial needs, I decided to make a list of all the times He had intervened on our behalf. The first thing that came to mind was something that happened when I was only fourteen years old and still living at home.

Unbeknown to me, my parents had loaned their grocery money to a needy family who failed to repay it, leaving us without groceries and no way to buy any. Just that morning Mom had informed Dad that there wasn't any food in the house. None! Of course, I had no idea how dire the situation was when Mom asked me to watch my siblings while they ran errands.

They had only been gone a few minutes when the doorbell rang. Opening the door I found myself face-to-face with Sister Ford, my Sunday school teacher. Without giving me a chance to say anything she asked, "Are your parents home?"

When I shook my head "no," she said, "Well, it doesn't matter. The Lord woke me up this morning about five o'clock and told me to buy your family a bill of groceries. Get your brother and help me carry these groceries in."

The backseat of her car was stacked with sacks of groceries and by the time Don and I finished carrying them in, the kitchen table was covered and sacks of groceries were spilling over on the kitchen counters. We thanked her profusely and begged her to stay until Dad and Mom returned but she wouldn't hear of it.

Thinking about that experience these many years later, I can almost hear God say, *"Trust Me. I will take care of you. I know what you need even before you ask."*

Now my mind leaps ahead several years to a Christmas Eve in Holly, Colorado. Brenda and I were just "kids"— she was twenty, and I was one year older— serving our first church. It was a small fellowship, numbering less than thirty members, located in the farming community of Holly, Colorado. It had been a lean year and financially things were tight. If the truth be known, we were flat broke and there wasn't a way in the world we could afford gifts for those we loved.

As I stood before the window in my small study, brooding over our unhappy plight, I recalled a scene from Truman Capote's little book, *A Christmas Memory*.[27] Seven-year-old Buddy and his distant cousin, a white-haired woman of sixty something, with whom he lives, are making Christmas gifts. Suddenly she looks up, her bright eyes gleaming, and says with a frightful intensity, "It's bad enough in life to do without something you want; but confound it, what gets my goat is not being able to give somebody something you want them to have."

That same feeling, or its close kin, churned in my chest. A flannel nightgown was what I wanted to buy Brenda and a fuzzy housecoat to keep her warm against the winter cold, which had a way of finding every crack in that old parsonage. Earlier, when we still had hopes of a Christmas windfall, she had mentioned how nice it would be to have one.

Of late, she had concerned herself with other things, like Christmas decorations which we already had from last year. Beneath her determined gaiety, though, I sensed her disappointment. Not about the nightgown, she could do without that. What troubled her was not being able to purchase gifts for those she loved.

It was already dark when someone knocked on the front door. Inviting Clifford Hart, a local rancher who also served as the county commissioner, into the living room Brenda called for me. She offered him a cup of coffee but he declined saying he could only stay a minute. Reaching inside his coat he extracted a check and handed it to me.

"What's this?" I asked.

"It's a check from the Co-op," he explained, "for your wheat."

"But I don't have any wheat," I protested.

Laughing he said, "Delight and I found some that you didn't know anything about and I sold it for you."

With that he bid us a merry Christmas and departed. We stood on the porch in the cold and watched him drive away. When the taillights of his Cadillac disappeared around the corner we shut the door. Unfolding the check I nearly fainted when I saw that it was for $220.00. That may not sound like much to you but in 1968 it represented a month's salary to us.

Thinking about that experience these many years later I can almost hear God say, *"Trust Me. I will take care of you. I know what you need even before you ask."*

In 1980 we accepted the call to become pastors of Christian Chapel in Tulsa, Oklahoma. It was a huge step of faith for us. We would be taking a significant reduction in salary and there was a good chance it would take some months for our home in Craig, Colorado, to sell. Still we felt this was the will of the Lord, so we moved to Tulsa.

The next twelve months were exhilarating and exhausting. The ministry was deeply fulfilling but the financial pressure was relentless. By August my patience was wearing thin. Part of my Scripture reading for August 10, 1981, was Psalm 22. Verse 1 says, "My God, my God, why hast thou forsaken me? Why art thou so far from helping me…"(KJV).

That was exactly how I felt and in frustration I poured out my soul on the pages of my journal:

"My God, why have You not sold my house in Craig and why must I suffer this financial loss? You sold Gordon and Linda's house, Dale and Betty Jo's house so why haven't You sold ours?

My God, why haven't You found us another home? Look how miraculously You provided for Ron and Linda so why haven't You provided for us?

My God, why haven't You sustained our automobiles? You know we don't have money to repair them yet they continue to self-destruct. Why haven't You provided us with a new car? We could afford one if we didn't have to

*pay two house payments. You provided
a new car for Richard and Sharon so
why don't You provide one for us?*

*My God, why haven't You sustained
our health? We trust in You. First it was
Leah, then me, and now Brenda and
the medical bills are running in the
hundreds of dollars.*

*My God, why have You listened to my
complaint? Why haven't You struck me
down? I'm ashamed. Forgive my imper-
tinence. We have trusted in You and
You have provided for us.*

*You have provided a house in Tulsa for
us at reduced rent and You have made
it possible for us to make our house
payments in Colorado. Thank You for
Your faithful provision.*

*I trust You to provide a miracle here as
well. Let me not complain or try to*

*manipulate the church board into helping
us. You are our source, our sufficiency!*

*I trust You to provide a miracle of a
new car. I specifically ask for it by
October 4, 1981."*

"Our fathers trusted in thee: they
trusted, and thou didst deliver them"
(Psalm 22:4 KJV).

Almost immediately we saw the hand
of God at work. We received a contract on
our home in Colorado and found a home
in Broken Arrow that would meet our
needs. On Friday, October 2, we closed on
our home in Colorado and on the following Monday we closed on our new home
in Broken Arrow. In between, on Sunday,
October 4th, we celebrated our first
anniversary as pastors of Christian
Chapel. The congregation presented us

with a check for $1,000.00 and the keys to a 1981 Oldsmobile Cutlass.

Thinking about that experience these many years later I can almost hear God say, *"Trust Me. I will take care of you. I know what you need even before you ask."*

In short order, I recalled several more times when God provided for us in special ways. In fact, I filled several pages in my journal just listing them. When I finished reviewing them I was greatly encouraged. Considering the many times He had provided for us in special ways, I could only conclude that God cared more about our needs than even our most caring friends. I didn't need to ask them for help. God was our source. He had proven Himself faithful in the past and I was confident that He would do so again.

Within a week I received a telephone call from a businessman I knew casually.

He asked if the ministry had any special financial needs. When I responded in the affirmative he said the Lord had impressed him to give the ministry a $5,000.00 dollar donation. A couple of days later, I received a check in the mail from an attorney who had heard me minister. He enclosed a note saying the Lord had impressed him to send the ministry a $1,000.00 donation. A month later, I walked into a retreat center to begin a men's retreat when a man came up to me and handed me a check for $1,000.00. He told me that the Lord had spoken to him several weeks earlier to give the ministry an offering, but since he didn't know where to send it he had just held onto the check until I arrived.

Thinking about that experience these many years later I can almost hear God say, *"Trust Me. I will take care of you. I know what you need even before you ask."*

Maybe you're facing a financial challenge right now. Instead of focusing on what you need, let me encourage you to remember how God has provided for you in the past. Prayers that focus primarily on our needs seldom build up our faith, while prayers which focus on God's character and faithfulness strengthen us. Even if our circumstances don't immediately change, we are still encouraged as we remember how God has taken care of us in the past.

Once you are centered in God's past faithfulness, once you have strengthened your faith by focusing on His goodness, I want you to make your needs known. Pray specifically and pray boldly. God is able to do more than you can ask or even imagine.[28] Get ready. He is about to open the windows of Heaven and pour out a blessing you can't contain![29]

Chapter 7

THANK GOD FOR
GRANDMA MILLER

The longer I live, the more I realize just how fortunate I have been. In addition to a very positive relationship with both my parents, as well as my brothers and sister, I was blessed with an extended family of loving grandparents, aunts, and uncles. Although I was never given any reason to think myself better than anyone else, I never doubted my worth as a person either. Within the extended family circle I knew I had a place. I was loved. I was somebody.

A key figure in my young world was Grandma Miller. Although her entire life was lived on the ragged edge of poverty, she was rich in spirit. She stood 4'11" with tightly-curled red hair. As a child I never realized she colored it, but she must have, because it remained the same tint until the day she died.

As I think about her now, she seems like something out of *Reader's Digest's* unforgettable characters. She was born in 1887 in a small village in Iowa, to a poor but hard-working family. Having little use for what they called "book learnin'," her parents put her to work in the sawmill when she was just seven years old. Consequently, she never learned to read or write, and could barely scribble her own name. As a child, I remember watching her struggle to sign her old-age pension check with an indelible pencil.

At the age of thirteen, still just a wisp of a girl, not quite five feet tall, she married James Lewis Miller. Thirteen years her senior, he was a big, strapping man, standing three inches over six feet and weighing nearly 260 pounds, with hands the size of hams. The early years of their life together were spent working for the railroad. Grandpa was a foreman, overseeing a crew laying track across Kansas. When the work ran out they settled in Greeley, Colorado. In 1910 they homesteaded in the sand hills near Merino, in the northeastern part of the state. After the depression they sold out and moved to the county seat where they took up residence in a poorer section of town.

Being her first grandchild, I was always welcome in Grandma's world—a world of braided rag rugs, coal oil stoves, and friends from "the old country." Grandma

was Dutch, but she lived in a neighbor-
hood of Russian immigrants; consequently, I was exposed to a culture
different from my own and to people who
spoke with a strange accent (that is, when
they didn't lapse into their mother
tongue). Grandma loved those old people
and so did I. I could sit by her side for
most of an afternoon listening as they
talked of people and places of which I
knew absolutely nothing. Sometimes I
slipped outside and picked honeysuckle
flowers, marveling at the tiny droplets of
sweetness they deposited on my tongue.

Grandpa died when I was ten years old
and I began spending four or five nights a
week with Grandma. She never really
trusted electricity so we seldom used it.
After dark we lit the kerosene lamps and
talked for hours. I can't remember much
of what was said, no special words of

wisdom, but I do remember feeling loved.
Grandma had a way of making me feel like
there wasn't anything I couldn't do. As I
recall those memories now, I realize that
Grandma accepted me as her peer while
allowing me to be a child when I needed
to be. Because of her, I had the best of
both worlds—adult company and accept-
ance, plus the freedom of childhood.

There were those who considered her
a bit eccentric in her later years. In truth,
she was just a throwback to an earlier age.
One time I asked her why she carried a
loaded pistol and brass knuckles in her
purse. Without batting an eye she said,
"Because if I ever get mad enough to kill
someone, I don't want to change my mind
while I hunt around for something to do
it with!"

Looking back now, these many years
later, I think her bark was worse than her

bite. I mean, I never knew her to harm anyone, and she was generous to a fault. Still, she did carry that pistol in her purse.

I gave up many childhood activities with my friends in order to spend time with her and I can say without a doubt that it was worth it. Only Grandma knows what personal interests and projects she let go unpursued so she could give me her undivided attention but, considering how much time she invested in me, I can only conclude that her sacrifice must have been significant. She guided me, she modeled her values for me, but she never tried to change me. In her presence I was never afraid of being judged or rejected. Her unconditional love gave me the security to be my real self.

Although she has been dead for more than forty years now, she lives on in my memory, and her influence shapes me

still. She taught me the value of relation-
ships. Under her gentle guidance I learned
to experience my deepest feelings and to
share them with those I love. She was
tenacious, and from her example I learned
to "hang tough" and finish what I started.
She believed in me and taught me to
believe in myself. I am who I am today, at
least in part, because of the investment
she made in me.

I wish there were some way to repay
her for all the love she poured into me. As
a boy I simply accepted it, never realizing
how rare and wonderful it really was,
never thinking to give her thanks. Now it's
too late. The best I can do is to try to live
in a way that honors her memory. And I
can pass her love on. I can do my best to
be the same kind of special friend to my
grandchildren that she was to me. It's all I

can do. I hope it's enough. Knowing her, I'll bet it's exactly what she had in mind.

Let me encourage you to take a moment right now and remember the people who have made a difference in your life—a coach, a Sunday school teacher, a college professor, an uncle or an older sibling, maybe even a kindly grand-parent. What did they do? How did they express their love? What were some of the things they did that made you feel special?

Chances are you took that relationship for granted never realizing how rare it was. And you probably didn't take the time to verbalize your gratitude either; I know I didn't, not to Grandma and not to God. I would give almost anything if I could go back and tell Grandma what her love meant to me, but I can't. Maybe you can. Maybe you can send an e-mail or write a letter or even a text message to those who have made a difference in your life. If it's possible, do it now before life's busyness pushes it from your mind. And give God thanks too, for He is the giver of every good gift.

Thank You, God, for Grandma Miller! And thank you, Grandma. I am a better person because of you.

Chapter 8

THANK GOD IN THE HARD TIMES

Leaving the RCA Dome I turned toward the hotel, depression dogging my steps. I should have felt exhilarated, or at least deeply satisfied, but I didn't. Being one of the speakers at the annual Bill Gaither Praise Gathering was a high honor, one I never expected to have; still, all I felt in the aftermath of my second session was an aching emptiness. The sessions had gone well enough, with lots of positive affirmation, but I couldn't seem to wring any joy out of the experience.

For the better part of two years I had been living in a fog. Somehow I managed to minister with surprising effectiveness, but nothing I did touched the sadness that was slowly sucking life out of me. Day after day I forced myself to go through the motions, desperately hoping this would be the day some light returned to my gray world, but it never happened. Instead the gloom seemed to deepen, causing me to doubt if I would ever again know the joy that had once characterized my life.

In Dante's *Inferno*, the writer takes a walk and suddenly finds himself disoriented, and so begins his journey into the various levels of hell with these words: "In the middle of the journey of our life I found myself in a dark wood."

That best describes what happened to me—in the middle of my own journey, I unexpectedly found myself in a dark wood. I was blindsided by a devastating loss, people I loved were hurting badly, and I couldn't seem to help them or myself. Week after week the darkness deepened and I found myself fearing it would never end.

Reminding myself that I was not the first person to walk this path helped some, but the pain was unrelenting. I took what courage I could from the knowledge that this dark place, though unfamiliar to me, was not unfamiliar to those who had gone before me. Many who walked this way will remain anonymous but others are well-known figures. For instance, Elijah the prophet found himself in a wood so dark he despaired of life and prayed to die.[30] Even Jesus was tempted to despair and on at least one occasion He confessed that His soul was "exceeding sorrowful even unto death."[31]

In classic devotional literature these experiences came to be known as the dark night of the soul and were considered a nearly universal experience. Sometimes, as in my case, the darkness descended as a result of a grievous loss, but at other times it seemed to come for no apparent reason. Whatever the cause, the darkness, along with the numbing sadness it brings, can be debilitating, especially if it continues for any length of time.

The fact that I tried to mask my pain, carefully concealing it beneath a facade of normalcy, probably complicated my situation. Still, I didn't know what else to do, not wanting to burden anyone else with my troubles. Thus I found myself walking the streets of Indianapolis in the deepening dusk, a sharp wind tugging at the collar of my jacket, while sorrow gnawed a hole in my heart.

City noise—the blaring of car horns, the rumble of a dump truck leaving a nearby construction site, raucous laughter spilling out of a bar as the after-work crowd unwound—clamored for my attention but I was mostly oblivious to it. I had ears only for the mournful voices within. Self-blame and bitter regret mingled, tempting me to despair. If only I had been a better friend. If only I had been a more faithful intercessor. If only I....

Nearing the hotel I paused, not yet ready to don my game face. Brenda and friends were waiting to go to dinner but I couldn't face them, not yet. Staring, with unseeing eyes, at my reflection in the plate glass window I felt a stirring deep within— a sense, too subtle to be described, yet too real to be denied. My throat got tight and I teared up. Unexpectedly I sensed God's presence, something I hadn't felt since this whole thing started.

Suddenly I found myself praying under my breath, silently telling God that I could endure anything as long as He was with me. What I couldn't bear was the thought that He had abandoned me. Yielding myself to His presence, I clung to His nearness as if my life depended upon it, for surely it did, whether I realized it or not.

It didn't last more than a minute or two, then the darkness closed around me again. Yet, in that unexpected moment of grace, a tiny hope was born. Like the first hint of spring it promised better things to come. In the dark days ahead I returned to it again and again. I knew the tragic things that had rent my life couldn't be undone but my well-being was no longer dependent upon that. God was my hope, the source of my life. He would restore my joy, of that I was sure. Like Elijah I had heard the "still small voice"[32] and it spoke life to me.

My depression didn't miraculously disappear, nor did the things that had caused me so much pain suddenly resolve themselves, but I found my strength somehow renewed. Day after day I put one foot in front of the other, pushing my way through the darkness, always drawing strength from that moment of grace. Like Paul, a man familiar with this dark wood, I learned that the strength of Christ is made perfect in my weakness.

Thank God I am no longer wandering in the "dark wood" but I have to admit that there are times when I long to relive that moment of grace, that moment when God suddenly felt nearer to me than the breath I breathed and more real than life itself. I pray I never return to that dark place, but I also realize it may be impossible to experience the fullness of God's grace except in times of extreme difficulty.

Maybe that is why James wrote, "Consider it pure joy, my brothers, whenever you face trials of many kinds, because you know that the testing of your faith develops perseverance. Perseverance must finish its work so that you may be mature and complete, not lacking anything."[33] Or as one notable Bible teacher said, "God allows hard things to happen **to** us in order to do something **in** us so that He can do something **through** us."

Christianity does not make us immune to the vicissitudes and sufferings so common to this life, but it does empower us to live with meaning in the midst of unspeakable loss. Therefore I will thank Him in the hard times, knowing "…that in all things God works for the good of those who love him, who have been called according to his purpose."[34]

My brother told me about a missionary's teenage daughter who was stricken with a grievous disease. Her digestive system stopped working and she was literally starving to death. To keep her alive the doctors inserted a shunt and began feeding her intravenously. Her activities were severely restricted and she had to carry a feeding pouch at all times. With no hope of a cure it was a heartbreaking situation but she managed it with surprising grace, trusting Jesus minute by minute to strengthen her.

After a couple of years the Lord instantaneously healed her. Overnight she was able to resume a normal life. Some months later she told her father, "I'm eternally grateful for my healing but there are times I miss the relationship I had with

Jesus when I was so sick. He was my only hope and I clung to Him for dear life."

Although I've never faced anything like that, I think I know what she was talking about. As I look back over my life it is the hard times I remember most clearly and it is there that God has revealed Himself to me in life-changing ways, howbeit His presence was seldom easy to discern. I do not court hard times but neither do I flee from them. Even as God spoke to Job out of the storm,[35] so does He speak to us, assuring us of His love and the promise of His presence. Therefore I will not fear no matter how dark the wood and I will thank Him in the hard times.

Chapter 9

THANK GOD FOR
SECOND CHANCES

At the age of twenty-three I was
called to be the pastor of First Assembly
of God in Florence, Colorado, at that time
one of the better churches in the Rocky
Mountain District. It was heady stuff for a
novice pastor and I soon fell prey to the
deadliest of all ministerial temptations—
pride. Almost without realizing it I began
to think more highly of myself than I
should have. From a child I had been
taught that "Pride goes before destruction,
and a haughty spirit before a fall,"[36] but I

———

never thought it could happen to me. Unfortunately, like Humpty Dumpty, I had a great fall and not all the king's horses or all the king's men could put this broken man back together again.

Here's what happened. I began to reason that with a ministry gift like mine it was a shame to limit my ministry to one congregation. I was convinced that the Holy Spirit wanted me to share my gift with the world and after fifteen months in Florence I resigned the pastorate and launched into evangelistic ministry. Had I been older and wiser I would have known that my reasoning was flawed. The only gift the Holy Spirit wants to share with the world is Jesus.

Initially things went very well. Several significant churches invited me to preach crusades and the Lord moved in remark-able ways, which only served to exacerbate my haughty spirit. Of course "God opposes the proud"[37] so it was just a matter of time before things began to fall apart. There is nothing to be gained by rehashing the messy details, so let me just say that I experienced some painful disappointmens, not to mention devastating rejection, and soon found myself without a place to preach.

In order to provide for my wife and infant daughter I worked in the hay fields of southeastern Colorado. When that work ran out we returned to Houston, Texas, where we moved in with Brenda's parents. Once again I found temporary work loading one hundred pound bags of rice into the belly of ships at the Port of Houston. It was backbreaking work especially given that it was July with both the temperature and the humidity climbing to nearly one hundred. After that I spent some days roofing houses in Idaho and by October I had a bit part in a Hollywood movie called *Brothers O'Toole*. It was being filmed at Buckskin Joe's, a restored western town located on the Royal Gorge near Canon City, Colorado.

We were nearly destitute and managed to hang on only because some friends took pity on us and invited us to live with them for a while. Brenda cleaned the house and baby-sat their infant son to help pay part of the rent. I was mostly gone, leaving the house early in the morning to go to the movie set and returning home late at night after the Belvedere Bar and Grill finally closed.

Night after night I sat in the bar feeling sorry for myself. I still felt called to the ministry but there didn't seem to be anyplace for me in the church. I loved God, but I no longer trusted Him. To my way of thinking He had let me down. Proverbs 19:3 says, "A man's own folly ruins his life, yet his heart rages against the Lord" and that's exactly what I was doing. My own pride and foolishness had destroyed my ministry and yet I was blaming God. Of course, I couldn't see it at the time.

As the weeks passed I grew more and more depressed. Day after day I would sit on the movie set comparing the illusion of movie making with the reality of ministry, especially the reality of the ministry we had experienced in our first pastorate in Holly, Colorado. During our three-year tenure several people had been gloriously saved, among them Bob and Diane. Following their conversion God restored their marriage and Brenda and I were privileged to spend the next two years mentoring them in the ways of the Lord.

Holy Communion was especially important to Bob and almost every week Brenda and I shared the Lord's Supper with them in their home. Each week Diane baked a small loaf of homemade bread, which she placed on a scarred coffee table in their living room along with four plastic cups. After filling the cups with grape juice all four of us would get down on our knees and Bob and Diane would pour out their hearts to Jesus in confession and repentance. Finally, we took communion and week after week the presence of the Holy Spirit filled their living room, turning it into a sanctuary, a holy place.

In my deepening depression I hungered to experience something like that again and one day I simply walked off the movie set and I never went back. In town I started throwing our things into suitcases, informing Brenda that we were going to Bob and Diane's. "But we don't know where they live," she protested. "They've moved and we haven't talked to them in more than two years."

Undeterred, I continued to pack our suitcases. "We'll find them," I said, "we have to."

After making a half a dozen phone calls and driving for more than eight hours we finally located them. They were living in a farmhouse in southwestern Kansas and when they saw us it was like we had never been apart. Two days later, on the last Saturday in November, 1972, Diane baked bread and I bought a bottle of grape juice. After putting the children to bed the four of us went into the living room where we gathered around the scarred coffee table that loomed so large in my memory.

The old farmhouse creaked and groaned in the cold as the wind howled, whipping up a high plain's blizzard. Inside the floor furnace wheezed as it fought to hold its own against the November night but I hardly noticed so intent was I on the task at hand. Carefully I filled the four plastic cups with grape juice before picking up the bread, still warm from the oven.

Kneeling there a wave of memories washed over me. In an instant, I was back in Holly, Colorado, in Bob and Diane's doublewide trailer house. Gone was the craziness of the past three years. Gone was my foolishness and pride. Gone was my hurt and disappointment. All washed away in the memory of an earlier time, a time when love and grace had made all things new.

Always before when we shared communion I heard their confession, but on this night the three of them heard mine and when I finished we were all crying— tears of remorse and tears of joy. Although the Lord would have been well justified in washing His hands of me, He did not. Instead of rejecting me God restored me. As far as the east is from the west so far did He remove my sins from me.[38]

With trembling hands I finally broke the bread, realizing as never before that it truly was my sins, my disobedience, and my rebellion that had broken His body. The Sanhedrin may have unjustly condemned Him and delivered Him to Pontius Pilate.[39] His own countrymen may have screamed for His blood.[40] Roman soldiers may have driven the nails,[41] but it was my sins that crucified Him!

After the bread I took the cup and said, "In the same manner Jesus gave them the cup, saying, 'This is my blood of the covenant, which is poured out for many for the forgiveness of sins.'"[42]

As we received communion that night a miracle happened in that old farmhouse, a miracle of grace and forgiveness, a miracle that continues to this very day. What all the king's horses and all the king's men couldn't do, the King's Son did. He put this broken man back together again. He gave me a second chance!

Have you lost your way; have you made some bad decisions; have you hurt those you love most? Are you trapped in a secret life, living a lie? Are you a stranger to your spouse and estranged from your children? Don't despair. All is not lost. What Jesus did for me in a farmhouse in Kansas more than thirty-five years ago, He will do for you!

I had to stop blaming others and take responsibility for my sinful choices and you will have to do the same. There are no extenuating circumstances, no self-justifying rationale that can excuse your sins. It is your fault! You are to blame and your only hope of deliverance is to throw yourself on the mercies of God.

The good news is that God's mercies are always greater than our sins.[43] "He does not treat us as our sins deserve or repay us according to our iniquities"[44] and there is nothing, absolutely nothing, that can separate from His love.[45] If you will call upon the Lord He will deliver you. He will forgive your sins and heal your hurts. He will do for you what He did for me. He will give you a second chance!

Why not pray this prayer with me right now. "Lord Jesus, I have sinned and made a mess of my life. I have hurt those I love most. I cannot save myself. You are my only hope. Forgive my sins, heal my heart and give me another chance. In Your holy name I pray. Amen."

If you prayed that prayer by faith, I declare on the authority of God's Word that your sins are forgiven. Romans 10:9, 10, and 13 says, "That if you confess with your mouth, 'Jesus is Lord,' and believe in your heart that God raised him from the dead, you will be saved. For it is with your heart that you believe and are justified, and it is with your mouth that you confess and are saved…for, 'Everyone who calls on the name of the Lord will be saved.'"

Now together let's thank God for second chances!

Chapter 10

THANK GOD FOR
HIS FAITHFULNESS

Outside my office window the sun is sparkling off the crystal clear waters of Beaver Lake on this the last day of the year. Earlier this morning the lake was shrouded in fog but the sun has washed it away and I can see clearly now. As I scan the lake I can't help reflecting, not only on the past year, but on the past forty-one years. Given our humble beginnings I would never have imagined that we could have ended up here, that is until I remember the dreams God placed in my heart when I was just a young man—dreams that He has been faithful to fulfill.

When Brenda and I were newlyweds and just starting out in the ministry, we spent nearly a year and a half preaching revival meetings in country churches from Cuero, Texas, to Post Falls, Idaho, and a half a hundred places in between. We spent hours in the car together, driving from one small church to the next. Sometimes Brenda read to me but more often than not we just talked. That is, I talked while Brenda mostly listened, being a person given to few words.

Mile after mile I regaled her with dreams about our future together. Someday, I told her, we are going to live in a cabin, on the side of a mountain, overlooking a lake. I will write books and preach in churches large and small all over the world. Someday I will have a national radio broadcast and be invited to preach at District Councils and camp meetings. Someday….

She would smile and listen politely but I could tell she didn't really believe me and who could blame her given our limited circumstances. In the course of time my dreams were mostly forgotten as we immersed ourselves in the work of the ministry, serving churches in Colorado, Texas, and Oklahoma. I began writing and published my first two books while serving the Church of the Comforter in Craig, Colorado.

In 1980 we became senior pastors of Christian Chapel in Tulsa, Oklahoma, and the Lord impressed me to give up writing for a season and concentrate on serving the church. For nearly seven years I did not write a thing for publication and I sometimes wondered if I would ever write again.

During those seven years God did many remarkable things at Christian Chapel and our congregation grew from barely one hundred people to more than a thousand. We purchased property and built our first facility. God granted me favor with the seminary at Oral Roberts University and I was frequently invited to lecture there. I also served as a group leader in the Field Education program at the seminary.

Through a truly remarkable series of events God brought me into contact with a radio executive whose vision helped me launch a nationwide via satellite call-in radio program called *Straight from the Heart*. Because Christian Chapel was an exceptionally strong missionary church, I began receiving invitations from missionaries to minister in a number of foreign countries. Almost without me realizing it, the Lord was fulfilling the dreams He had put into my heart when I was just a young man starting out in ministry.

In the spring of 1987 Honor Books approached me about writing four books for them. They had heard my radio broadcasts and felt that I would be a good fit for their publishing house. Of course, I was excited but I had to pray about it. In 1980 the Lord had told me not to write until He released me and I did not want to be disobedient. After three weeks I felt released to write again and I signed a contract with Honor Books. Over the next five years I published seven books with them including *The Making of a Man,* which was a finalist in the Devotional category for the Gold Medallion Book of the year.

In 1991 Brenda and I bought a small acreage on Beaver Lake as a twenty-fifth wedding anniversary gift to ourselves. We resigned from Christian Chapel a year later and with the help of Brenda's parents we built a small cabin overlooking the lake. I planned to write each morning and when I completed my day's work I would cut firewood or go fishing. Brenda would prepare healthy home-cooked meals, catch up on her reading, and indulge her penchant for crafts.

At that time the nearest paved road was nine miles away and the closest town three times that far. Carroll Electric Cooperative brought power to the property but we had to provide our own water and sewer system. Subsequently we drilled a well and put in a septic system. The first two years were nearly idyllic. Without telephone service or television it was almost like going back in time. On long winter evenings we read by the wood-burning stove, played table games, or just talked. Sometimes we chose to chat with only a kerosene lamp for light in memory of my Grandma Miller.

By the second year we had telephone service, if you can call a four-party line telephone service. We had a private telephone line and satellite television by the third year and shortly thereafter the internet. Now we are much better informed but not nearly as content. Although we live in the woods, the internet and satellite television have brought the world right to our door.

Fifteen years ago when I left the pastorate and moved to the lake, I thought my ministry would be primarily writing. Boy, was I wrong. Although I've written 22 books in the last fifteen years, I've also traveled almost 2 million miles and preached more than 2,500 times. Now

we've added ministry on the internet
(www.RichardExleyMinistries.org) with
podcasts and a bi-weekly blog and the
beat goes on!

Why do I tell you all of this? Because I
want you to see how God's faithfulness
manifests itself in an ordinary life. I'm no
one special and neither is Brenda, except
to me. What God has done for us, He will
do for you. The Lord would have been
well justified had He given up on me any
number of times during the last forty
years, especially during the early years, but
He refused. Even though my faith failed
on occasion, He has always remained
faithful for He cannot deny Himself.[46]

Take a moment now and examine
your own life. What God-given dreams
has the Lord placed in your heart? I'm not
talking about personal ambitions but
dreams birthed by the Spirit. Dr. Jim

Horvath, a personal friend of mine, carried a God-given dream of ministering in the Philippines in his heart for nearly twenty years before the Lord brought it to fruition. Now he has one of the most effective evangelistic ministries to the islands. What God has done for Jim, He will do for you!

Don't look at your circumstances or you may despair. You may feel that you simply do not have the wherewithal to see your God-given dreams become reality or you may feel that your willful disobedience has disqualified you. Either way you will be tempted to discard your dreams. Instead, look to God for He is the author and finisher of our faith[47] and He who has begun this good work in you is faithful to bring it to completion.[48]

Nearly twenty years ago I was facing some unusual challenges. It seemed I had reached a stalemate in my life and ministry. After several years of remarkable growth the church I was serving had reached a plateau. No matter what I did, we seemed stuck. To complicate matters a small, but vocal group, were critical of my leadership. On top of everything else my latest book was not selling nearly as well as anticipated. As a result I was experiencing some doubts regarding the effectiveness of my ministry.

One morning, during my devotional time, I was reading in the Psalms when I came across Psalm 138:7 and 8. I had read that passage numerous times before but that particular morning the words seemed to leap off the page. "Though I walk in the midst of trouble, you preserve my life; you stretch out your hand against the anger of my foes, with your right hand you save me. **The Lord will fulfill his purpose**

for me; your love, O Lord, endures forever—do not abandon the works of your hands" (emphasis added).

Although my situation did not immediately change I was at peace. God had spoken to me through His Word. No matter what others did He would fulfill His purpose in my life! Not necessarily my goals and ambitions, but His purpose, those God-given dreams He had placed in my heart and that was enough.

As you think about your own God-given dreams remember His faithfulness and take heart. "This is what the Lord says: '...For I know the plans I have for you,' declares the Lord, 'plans to prosper you and not to harm you, plans to give you hope and a future.'"[49]

Brenda and I are living God's dream for our life, not because of our faith but because of His faithfulness, and so can you. "Trust in the Lord with all your heart and lean not on your own understanding; in all your ways acknowledge him, and he will make your paths straight."[50] That is, He will fulfill your God-given dreams!

Thank God for His faithfulness!

Note to the Reader

As you come to the end of this little book I want to encourage you to make a decision to live with a thankful heart from this day forward. Do that, "And the peace of God, which transcends all understanding, will guard your hearts and your minds in Christ Jesus" (Philippians 4:7). The first thing you can do is make your own "Golden List."

MY GOLDEN LIST

Finally, brothers, whatever is true, whatever is noble, whatever is right, whatever is pure, whatever is lovely, whatever is admirable—if anything is excellent or praiseworthy—think about such things.

—Philippians 4:8

1)

2)

3)

4)

5)

6)

7)

8)

9)

10)

Once you have completed your *Golden List,* take a moment to thank the Lord for

His blessings. Begin with today and work your way back through your life. Recall as many special moments as you can, giving God thanks for each and every one. Pay particular attention to the people who have touched your life through the years— a teacher, a special friend, a family member, a coach, a spouse, or even a pastor. They were not there by accident. God brought them into your life to strengthen and encourage you.

Living with a thankful heart means taking the time and effort to express our gratitude, not only to the Lord, but also to all the people who have enriched our lives. I'm thinking of a pastor who cared for my soul at a critical point in my life. Each Monday morning, for a year, he drove fifty miles across Houston in rush hour traffic so he could meet with me. His fingerprints are all over my life and I am eternally grateful to him and to the Lord. He's gone to be with the Lord, but he lives on in my heart; a giant of a man who took time for me. Without a doubt I'm a better man because of him.

You've probably thought of someone too, or maybe several people. Why don't you set aside some time right now to write a note or send an email thanking them for their investment in your life? Let them know that you wouldn't be the person you are today if they hadn't been there for you. Be specific. Let them know what they did that made a difference for you. Believe me, it will be time well invested.

ENDNOTES

1. Jim Stovall, *The Ultimate Gift* (David C. Cook Publishers, Colorado Springs, CO, Copyright 2001, 978-0781445634).

2. Ibid., p. 124.

3. Philippians 4:6–7.

4. Philippians 4:7 (KJV).

5. Romans 5:8.

6. See Matthew 27:45–46.

7. 2 Corinthians. 5:21.

8. See Psalm 103:10–11.

9. See Psalm 103:17 and Lamentations 3:22–23.

10. See John 3:17.

11. See John 3:16.

12. See 1 John 1:9.

13. See Hebrews 12:2.

14. See Romans 8:1.

15. See 2 Corinthians 5:21.

16. Psalm 103:1–4.

17. Isaiah 65:24.

18. Hebrews 4:16.

19. See Psalm 103:1–3, Isaiah 53:5, and James 5:14–15.

20. See Joshua 1:5 and Matthew 28:20.

21. 2 Corinthians 5:8.

22. Philippians 1:21.

23. John 14:3 (KJV).

24. Hebrews 5:4.

25 Isaiah 41:9-13.

26 Isaiah 41:9-10.

27 Truman Capote, *A Christmas Memory* (New York: Random House, Inc., 1996). Originally published in 1958 by Random House in *Breakfast at Tiffany's*.

28 Ephesians 3:20.

29 Malachi 3:10.

30 1 Kings 19:3–5.

31 Matthew 26:38 (KJV).

32 1 Kings 19:12 (KJV).

33 James 1:2-4.

34 Romans 8:28.

35 Job 38:1.

36 Proverbs 16:18.

37 James 4:6.

38 Psalm 103:12.

39 Matthew 27:1–2.

40 Matthew 27:25.

41 Mathew 27:31–37.

42 Matthew 26:28.

43 Romans 5:20.

44 Psalm 103:10.

45 Romans 8:35–39.

46 2 Timothy 2:13.

47 Hebrews 12:2.

48 Philippians 1:6.

49 Jeremiah 29:10-11.

50 Proverbs 3:5–6.

———

ABOUT THE AUTHOR

 **Richard Exley** is the author of thirty-one books, many of them best-sellers. Most recently *From Grief to Gratefulness* and *Man of Valor*. *The Making of a Man* was a finalist for the prestigious Gold Medallion Award.

His rich and diversified background has included serving as senior pastor of churches in Colorado and Oklahoma, as well as hosting several popular radio programs, including the nationally syndicated *Straight from the Heart*.

When not traveling the country as a speaker, Richard and his wife, Brenda Starr, spend their time in a secluded cabin over-looking picturesque Beaver Lake in north-west Arkansas.

Richard enjoys quiet talks with old friends, kerosene lamps, good books, a warm fire when it is cold, and a good cup of coffee anytime.

He's an avid Denver Bronco's fan, an aspiring bass fisherman, and an amateur photographer.

To write the author or to schedule speaking engagements, seminars, as well as mens' and couples' retreats, you can contact the author by visiting his website at: www.richard-exleyministries.org.

You are also invited to listen to the author's daily *Straight from the Heart* podcast, also available on his website or you may subscribe to them at *itunes*.

ENLARGE YOUR FAITH WITH OTHER GREAT BOOKS BY RICHARD EXLEY

The Alabaster Cross (A Novel)

The Alabaster Cross is a compelling page-turner but so much more. A deeply human story, it is filled with profound spiritual truths. Trapped in a world of anger, Bryan Whittaker cannot move on with his life until he takes a journey into his past ... a dangerous journey that will lead him into the heart of the Amazon Rain Forest. If you've ever struggled to restore a broken relationship you will identify with Bryan's journey as he strives to make peace with his past.

From Grief to Gratefulness

While honestly acknowledging the pain of losing a loved one, *From Grief to Gratefulness* affirms the truth of Scripture, the promise of eternal life and the comfort of God who is near in the time of loss. Ultimately it is an invitation to celebrate the precious gift of life.

Intimate Moments for Couples

Drawing upon the experience gleaned from more than four decades of marriage and ministry, Richard Exley shares practical wisdom and Scriptural insights to help couples experience the intimacy their hearts hunger for. His candor and conversational writing style make for an enjoyable read even as it provides wise counsel designed to make even the best marriage better.

Man of Valor

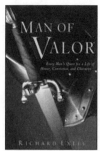

Don't measure your future by your past. God is about to intervene in your life and do a new thing. Using Scriptural principles and real life examples Richard Exley will show you how to become the man you were destined to be—a true man of valor.

Visit your local Christian Bookstore
or go online at
www.RichardExleyMinistries.org
to purchase your own copy.

If this book has touched your life,
we would like to hear from you.
Please write us at:
Vallew Press
P. O. Box 35327
Tulsa, Oklahoma 74153

VALLEW
PRESS